Old Testament Stories

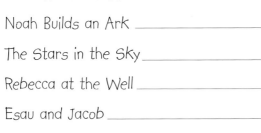

Written by Leena Lane   Illustrated by Roma Bishop

God Made the World

At the beginning of time, God made the world.

"Let there be light," God said. So light shone in the darkness.

God made the sky. God made clouds to float across the sky, winds to blow, thunder, and lightning, and rain.

God made the land and the wide oceans. God made plants of many kinds – tall trees, little flowers, juicy grapes and fruits, the prickly cactus, and velvety moss.

God made the scorching sun to shine in the day and the moon to glow at night. God made millions of twinkling stars. God was pleased with everything God had made.

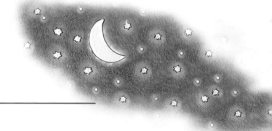

4

Then God said, "Let the seas be filled with creatures." Fish and creatures of all colors and shapes swam beneath the waves.

God said, "Let the air be filled with birds!" Parrots, swans, flamingoes, eagles, and birds of all sizes flapped their wings and flew.

God made all the animals. Reindeer, tall giraffes, strong elephants, and stripy raccoons... God made them all. And God was pleased with what God had made.

God still hadn't finished. God made people to be friends of God. God told them to look after the world – the plants and animals, birds and fish. And God was very pleased with everything God had made.

A LITTLE PRAYER

Thank you, Lord, for everything you made –
the whole world and everything in it.
And thank you for making me.

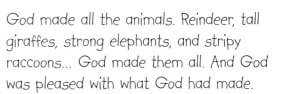

Noah Builds an Ark

Noah was a good man who loved God. But in the world there was trouble. God had made a wonderful world, but the people had spoilt everything. There was fighting everywhere.

God told Noah there would be a great flood. God would send it. Noah must build a boat and fill it with animals – two of every kind of animal on the earth. God would keep them safe when the flood came.

So Noah built a huge wooden boat called an ark. He covered it with tar to keep out the rain. It would float on the waters until the flood was over.

Noah collected two of every kind of animal and bird on the earth.

Noah packed food for his family and all the animals. They were ready for the day when the rain began and the rivers burst into flood. God promised to keep them safe.

The flood came and the people on the land were washed away. But the ark floated on the water. Noah and his family were safe inside, even though it was very noisy with all the animals!

Then after many weeks, it stopped raining. Dry land appeared again at last. Noah and his family thanked God for keeping them safe. All the animals were happy to come out of the ark!

God put a rainbow in the sky as a promise that there would never be a flood like that again.

A LITTLE PRAYER

Thank you, God, for keeping Noah safe in the flood. Thank you for watching over me too.

The Stars in the Sky

Abraham was a good man who loved God and did what God asked. God told him to leave his father's home to settle in a new land which God showed him.

God promised to make Abraham's family very important for many years to come. The problem was, Abraham and his wife Sarah could not have children. Without children, their family could not grow any bigger. But Abraham believed God's promise and waited.

One day, God told Abraham that he would have a son and a very large family.

"Look at the stars and try to count them," said God. "You will have as many people in your family as the number of stars you can see." Imagine how amazed Abraham felt about that!

Abraham grew to be an old man. Sarah still had no children. But Abraham trusted God and believed God's special promise.

When Abraham was ninety-nine years old, God's promise started to come true!

God gave Abraham and Sarah a son! They called him Isaac, which means "laughter." They were so pleased to have a baby at last! God had kept the promise.

A LITTLE PRAYER

Thank you, God, for keeping your promise to Abraham. Thank you that you will always look after me, too.

Rebecca at the Well

Abraham's son Isaac grew up. The time came for him to marry. Abraham sent a servant back to the land where Abraham first came from to find a girl to marry Isaac. It was a long journey.

The servant stopped at a well outside a city, where the women and girls fetched water every evening for their families. He asked God to help him.

"If one of the girls offers me and my camels a drink, then I will know she is the one you want to be Isaac's wife."

Every evening Rebecca fetched water from the well for her family. She collected it in a large water jar.

She noticed Abraham's servant standing at the well with ten camels. He looked tired and thirsty.

"Please give me a drink," he said.

Rebecca lowered the water jar from her shoulder and gave it to him to drink. When he had finished, she fetched some more water for the camels. It took a long time to get enough water for ten thirsty camels!

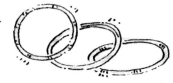

The servant was very pleased. He took a beautiful gold ring and gold bracelets out of his bag and put them on Rebecca. She had never seen anything so fine!

"Who is your father?" asked the servant. "Would there be room for me and my camels to stay at your father's house?" he asked.

"My father's name is Bethuel," said Rebecca. "There will be plenty of room at our house for you to stay." Bethuel was Isaac's cousin.

Rebecca ran home to tell her family about the man and the camels. The servant meanwhile praised God for showing him the girl that Isaac would marry.

The servant went to Rebecca's house and asked if Rebecca would go and be Isaac's wife. She agreed and set off the next day to marry Isaac. They were very happy.

A LITTLE PRAYER

Thank you, God, for listening to the servant's prayer and helping him to find Rebecca.

Thank you that you listen to me when I ask for help.

11

Esau and Jacob

Rebecca and Isaac were very happy. A few years later they had twins – two little boys!

Although Esau and Jacob were twin brothers, they were not at all alike. Esau had red hair. He was good at hunting and loved being outdoors.

Jacob was a quiet man who liked staying at home to help his mother. He loved cooking and could make delicious stews.

Esau was born first, which meant that when his father died, Esau would be given all that his father, Isaac, owned. Jacob secretly wanted to be the one to get this, so he planned to trick his brother.

One day, when Esau came home from hunting, he was very, very hungry. He could smell a delicious stew that Jacob had been cooking. It was Esau's favorite meal!

"Give me some of that stew," he asked Jacob.

"Only if you promise to let me be the one who gets Dad's land when he dies," said Jacob.

Esau couldn't resist the stew any longer, so he promised to let Jacob have all that their father owned. It would be as if Jacob was born first. Esau only cared about his hungry tummy!

Jacob was pleased at first that his trick had worked. But soon he became very sorry about it. Esau was his brother, after all. Many years later, Esau forgave Jacob and the brothers became friends again.

A LITTLE PRAYER

Thank you, God, that you helped Esau and Jacob to be friends again.

Thank you for our families; help us when we quarrel or are unkind to others.

Joseph and his Brothers

Jacob had twelve sons and one daughter. He loved them all, but Joseph was his favorite.

Jacob gave Joseph a very special present: a wonderful coat to wear. Joseph was very pleased, but his brothers were angry.

"Why does Dad love him more than us?" they muttered. "Why can't we all have a coat like that?"

They made a terrible plan to get rid of Joseph and threw him into an empty well. They were going to leave him there to die.

Suddenly they saw a group of men with camels on their way to Egypt.

"Let's sell Joseph to those men!" said Judah, one of the brothers.

So Joseph was sold to be a slave in Egypt. He thought he would never see his father or his brothers again. His father, Jacob, thought his favorite son was dead.

But God looked after Joseph. Time passed and he became the king's friend and an important leader in Egypt. Many years later, his brothers came to Egypt, asking for food. They did not recognize Joseph.

"Do my brothers remember how cruel they were to me?" thought Joseph. He found they were very sorry. So Joseph welcomed them and gave them food. Joseph's father, Jacob, was now a very old man. He was so happy to find his son alive. The family was together again at last.

A LITTLE PRAYER

Thank you that you looked after Joseph,
even when he was in trouble.
Thank you that you made things turn out right.

Moses, the River Baby

Miriam was very pleased – her mother had had a baby boy! Miriam had a new little brother. But her mother was afraid.

"Miriam," she whispered, "don't tell anyone about our baby. The King of Egypt has told his soldiers to take all the Hebrew baby boys and throw them into the river!"

So Miriam didn't tell anyone about her baby brother. It was a secret. But the baby soon grew. He cried very loudly! Miriam was afraid that someone might hear him...

But Miriam's mother had a good idea. She made a basket out of reeds and covered it with tar to keep out water. She put the baby in the basket and went down to the river bank. She put the basket in the reeds at the water's edge.

"Stay near by and watch," she said to Miriam. Miriam stayed near the basket and watched. She wondered what would happen to her little brother.

Suddenly Miriam heard a voice near the reeds. She saw the royal princess and her maidservants! The princess found the basket and picked up the baby.

"It's a baby!" she exclaimed. 'I will look after him and call him Moses."

Miriam crept out from her hiding place.

"I know who can feed him," she said to the princess. Then Miriam ran home to fetch her mother. The princess asked Miriam's mother to look after him until he was old enough to live at the royal palace.

God had kept Moses safe.

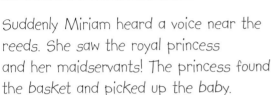

LITTLE PRAYER

Thank you, God, for keeping baby Moses safe. Thank you for watching over me while I sleep.

"I'm Listening, Lord"

Samuel was a boy who lived in the Temple. He had a very special job to do. He helped Eli the priest. Eli was very old and nearly blind.

One night when Samuel was asleep in bed, he heard a voice calling his name.

"Samuel! Samuel!" Samuel got up at once and ran to Eli.

"Here I am!" he said.

Eli was very surprised.

"I didn't call you. Go back to bed," he said.

So Samuel went back to bed and tried to go back to sleep.

"Samuel! Samuel!" called the voice again. At once Samuel jumped up and ran to Eli. "Here I am!" he said. "I didn't call you!" said Eli. "Go back to bed."

So Samuel went back to bed. Then he heard the voice for a third time. "Samuel! Samuel!" Samuel jumped out of bed again and ran to Eli.

"Here I am!" he said.

This time, Eli knew what was happening. It was God who was calling to Samuel!

"Next time he calls, you must say, 'Speak, Lord, your servant is listening.' Now go back to bed."

Samuel went back to bed. Samuel went back to bed.

"Samuel! Samuel!" called the voice again. This time, Samuel knew it was God.

"Speak, Lord, your servant is listening," said Samuel.

Samuel did listen, and God spoke to him. Samuel grew up able to guide the people in God's ways.

A LITTLE PRAYER

Thank you, God, that you speak to those who listen. Help me to listen to your voice and obey it.

David and the Giant

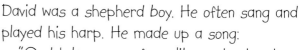

David was a shepherd boy. He often sang and played his harp. He made up a song:
"God takes care of me like a shepherd. God gives me everything I need."
Once a fierce bear attacked his sheep. David had no sword. He had only his shepherd's stick and his sling. David killed the bear.

One day, David's father sent him to see his brothers. They were in the army, ready to fight against the Philistines.

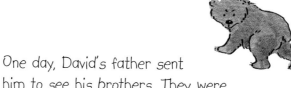

The Philistine army had a man called Goliath. He was very big and very strong.
"Send someone out to fight me!" he roared. But no one would go.

"I will go and fight that man," David said boldly. "I'm not afraid. God has saved me from lions and bears. I know God will save me again."

"All right," said the king. "But you must wear my armor and use my sword."

David tried on the king's armor, but it was too big and heavy. He took it off again. Then he went to the stream and picked up five smooth stones.

David went out to fight. Goliath roared with laughter.

"I'm going to kill you!" he shouted. David took one of the smooth round stones and put it in his sling. The stone hit Goliath and he fell to the ground.

David and his friends were safe, and they gave thanks to God.

A LITTLE PRAYER

David was very brave because you were with him.

Help me to trust you, too, Lord.

Elijah and the Ravens

Elijah was a man who listened to God. God told Elijah that there would be a terrible drought. No rain would fall for two or three years.

God told Elijah not to worry.

"Leave this place," said God, "and go east. Find a stream called Cherith and hide yourself there. You will be able to drink from the stream."

So Elijah walked many miles along the dusty roads.

At last, far away from his home, Elijah found the stream. He could drink the fresh, cool water whenever he felt thirsty. But Elijah had nothing to eat.

"Stay beside this stream," said God, "and I will send you food."

Suddenly Elijah looked up and saw something moving. It was a raven – a big black bird – carrying a piece of food in its beak! Then more ravens flew down, each with bread and meat for Elijah.

Each day, when he was hungry, the ravens brought him bread and meat. When Elijah was thirsty, he drank from the cool, fresh stream.

After a while, the stream started to dry up because there was no more rain. God told Elijah to go to another town where a woman would give him some food. Elijah thanked the ravens for bringing him food every day, then he set off down the dusty road again.

A LITTLE PRAYER

Thank you, Lord, for looking after Elijah.
Thank you for my food today.

The Little Servant Girl

There was once a little servant girl who lived far from home. Her mistress was kind to her. The little girl was worried about her master, Naaman. He was an important army leader. Sadly, he had a terrible illness which made his skin turn as white as snow. Nobody knew how to make him well.

The little servant girl knew about a man in her old homeland called Elisha.

"I wish Naaman could see Elisha," she said to her mistress. "I'm sure he could help make my master well again."

Naaman heard what the little servant girl said. So he went to ask the king if he could go and find Elisha. Naaman set off with his horses and chariot and stopped at the door of Elisha's house.

Elisha's servant came out and told Naaman to wash seven times in the River Jordan and he would be made well. Naaman didn't really want to wash in the river. It was dirty! How could that help? But his servants helped him. Naaman dipped himself in the river seven times...

... and he was made completely well again! His skin looked smooth and healthy.

"Thank you, God, for making me well again!" he said. He was glad he had listened to his little servant girl.

LITTLE PRAYER

Thank you, God, for making Naaman better.
Thank you for caring for me when I feel unwell.

Daniel and the Lions

Daniel was taken to live in a place called Babylon, far away from his home. But he knew that God was with him wherever he went. Daniel loved God and prayed to him.

Daniel worked hard and served the King.

One day the King had a dream which no one could understand. Only Daniel could tell the King what it meant. The King rewarded Daniel by making him a leader. He was given fine clothes to wear.

A new King called Darius came to Babylon. Daniel was still a leader, but Daniel's enemies plotted against him. They wanted to get rid of him.

King Darius had made a rule that people could only pray to the King, or they would be thrown into a pit of lions. But Daniel still prayed to God. He was arrested and taken to be fed to the lions!

The King was horrified. He hoped that Daniel would somehow survive. As soon as morning came, he went back to the lions' pit.
"Daniel! Has your God saved you?" he called.

Daniel called back, "Yes! I'm alive!"
God had sent an angel to stop the lions from hurting him. The King released Daniel and punished the men who had tried to hurt him. King Darius told everyone how wonderful God was for saving Daniel.

A LITTLE PRAYER

Lord, Daniel trusted you and you kept him safe from the hungry lions. Help me to trust you too.

Jonah Runs Away

God told Jonah to go to a city called Nineveh. The people who lived there were cruel and didn't do what God wanted. Jonah didn't want to go and speak to them. So he ran in the opposite direction.

He found a ship which was going to Spain. Jonah thought God wouldn't find him if he sailed far away.

But God sent a mighty storm and the sailors thought they would all drown. Jonah told the sailors that he had tried to run away from God.

"Throw me into the sea," said Jonah. "The storm will stop and you will be safe." The sailors didn't want to throw Jonah overboard; they tried to row with all their might. But the storm got worse.

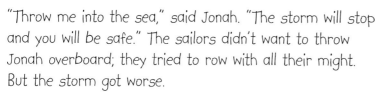

"Let's do what he says," said the sailors, and they threw Jonah into the sea. The storm stopped at once. The sailors were amazed. They thanked God for saving them.

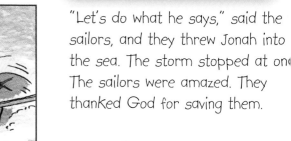

But Jonah didn't drown in the deep sea. God sent an enormous fish to come and swallow up Jonah.

Jonah lived inside the fish for three days and three nights. From inside the fish, Jonah thanked God for rescuing him at the bottom of the sea.

Then God told the fish to spit Jonah out on the shore. Again God told Jonah to go to Nineveh. This time, Jonah did what God said!

A LITTLE PRAYER

Thank you, God, for saving Jonah in the sea. Help me to do what you tell me and not run away from you.

Published in the United States of America by
Abingdon Press, 201 Eighth Avenue South, Nashville, Tennessee 37203

ISBN 0-687-06527-5

First edition 2003

Copyright © 2003 AD Publishing Services Ltd
1 Churchgates, The Wilderness, Berkhamsted, Herts HP4 2UB
Text copyright © 2003 AD Publishing Services Ltd, Leena Lane
Illustrations copyright © 2003 Roma Bishop

References for Bible stories
God Made the World: Genesis 1
Noah Builds an Ark: Genesis 6:9 - 8:17
The Stars in the Sky: Genesis 12, 15, 18, and 21
Rebecca at the Well: Genesis 24
Esau and Jacob: Genesis 25:19-34
Joseph and his Brothers: Genesis 37, 42-45
Moses, the River Baby: Exodus 2
"I'm Listening, Lord": 1 Samuel 3
David and the Giant: 1 Samuel 17
Elijah and the Ravens: 1 Kings 17:1-6
The Little Servant Girl: 2 Kings 5
Daniel and the Lions: Daniel 6
Jonah Runs Away: Jonah 1-4

Printed and bound in Singapore